EASY STYLE

300 DECORATING SHORTCUTS

Better Homes and Gardens® Books
Des Moines, Iowa

Better Homes and Gardens® Books
An imprint of Meredith® Books

Easy Style • 300 Decorating Shortcuts
Project Editor: Linda Hallam
Contributing Editors: Joetta Moulden, Elaine Markoutsas
Contributing Writer: Laura Collins
Art Director: Jerry J. Rank
Copy Editor: Carol Boker
Proofreaders: Sheila Mauck, Deb Smith
Editorial and Design Assistants: Jennifer Norris, Karen Schirm, Barbara A. Suk,
Production Director: Douglas M. Johnston
Production Manager: Pam Kvitne
Assistant Prepress Manager: Marjorie J. Schenkelberg

Meredith® Books
Editor in Chief: James D. Blume
Design Director: Matt Strelecki
Managing Editor: Gregory H. Kayko
Executive Shelter Editor: Denise L. Caringer

Director, Sales & Marketing, Retail: Michael A. Peterson
Director, Sales & Marketing, Special Markets: Rita McMullen
Director, Sales & Marketing, Home & Garden Center Channel: Ray Wolf
Director, Operations: Valerie Wiese

Vice President, General Manager: Jamie L. Martin

Better Homes and Gardens® Magazine
Editor in Chief: Jean LemMon
Executive Interior Design Editor: Sandra S. Soria

Meredith Publishing Group
President, Publishing Group: Christopher M. Little
Vice President, Consumer Marketing & Development: Hal Oringer

Meredith Corporation
Chairman and Chief Executive Officer: William T. Kerr

Chairman of the Executive Committee: E. T. Meredith III

Cover photograph: Colleen Duffley. The room is shown on *page 5*.

All of us at Better Homes and Gardens® Books are dedicated to providing you with information and ideas you need to enhance your home. We welcome your comments and suggestions about this book on stylish decorating shortcuts. Write to us at: Better Homes and Gardens Books, Shelter Department, RW–206, 1716 Locust St., Des Moines, IA 50309–3023.

EASY STYLE CONTENTS

IF YOU HAVE TIME TO ELEVATE A LAMP with books or throw a canvas cloth over a sofa, you have time to decorate. With today's comfortable, personal style, some of the most inviting decorating also is the quickest and simplest. Add a fashionable throw and bright oversize pillows to your sofa, group flea market architectural fragments or plates on a wall, stack baskets or old suitcases as a bedside table, bring the patio table inside, lean mirrors on the mantel, knot and hang sheer fabric on iron drapery rods.

GETTING STARTED

In Chapter 1, you'll find inspiration to help you get started with the basics of colors, backgrounds, and furniture. Turn to Chapter 2 if you like the idea of a room-by-room approach for quick ideas. Or, when you have only an afternoon, an hour, or even less, use Chapters 3 through 5 for quick fixes. To make it easy, tips are numbered from 1 through 300.

Filled with dried fruits, these urns illustrate the best of easy style. Collect urns for interesting shapes and character and elevate small ones with books. Arrange so urns or other objects form overlapping triangles; too much space dilutes impact.

THE WEEKEND STRETCHES BEFORE YOU. TAKE advantage of the time to accomplish projects that make a difference in how your home looks and lives. If you are beginning to decorate your home or a room or two, start with the basics. Can you work with the wall color? Do you have the key pieces of furniture for a comfortable room? Do you need to add a lamp, a table, or window treatments to make the space work for you? Do you have collections, family photographs, and books that make a room come alive? Would you like a room that changes with the seasons? Look for stylish ideas that do all this and much more. And, for more help with techniques, projects, and materials, turn to Chapter 5 for how-to directions, Have fun. That's what decorating is all about.

WEEKEND
WONDERS

Stylish Living Rooms

Cozy Family Spaces

Peaceful Master Retreats

Relaxing Baths

Collection-Filled Havens

Versatile All-Season Rooms

For instant chic, create a grouping with a double-skirted table (see page 100 for how-to directions) and padded invitation board (page 101). The striped invitation board ties the composition together with transition between the table and lamp.

WORK WITH YOUR NEUTRALS

Start with basic off-white or palest taupe walls and enjoy a blank canvas for your creativity. (Subtle hints of cream are warmer than stark white for walls.) Achieve this sophisticated look by purposefully limiting your colors and patterns. The white sofa mixes with both the slipcovered wing chair and the armchair with a recovered cushion seat. Shades of brown and rust and touches of black finish with style. For easier care, cover upholstered pieces in washable, white cotton duck slipcovers.

1-5

▦ *Substitute a painted tray and a grouping of plates for a large focal-point-creating piece of art. Search for these transferware-style plates in flea markets and antique stores. Don't worry about odd pieces; mixing sizes is part of the fun.*

▦ *Incorporate a scrap of needlepoint and fringe for one focal-point-creating pillow for your sofa. Vary the sizes and shapes of other pillows, but err on the large size (20 to 24 inches square); small pillows alone look underscaled.*

▦ *Keep your look light and open with glass-topped coffee and accent tables. Well-designed ones are available in every price range and style. If you have small children, avoid tables with exposed glass or sharp metal edges.*

▦ *Balance large pieces, such as an armoire, with equally tall pieces—here the ficus tree and the floor lamp.*

▦ *Edit your accessories for a sleek look. One unusually shaped bowl elevated on a stand is more dramatic and interesting than a number of small pieces. Fill with apples or pears for color.*

▓ *Think versatility. A chest of drawers works well as a lamp table in this cozy family sitting room—and who doesn't need more storage? For a small dining room, substitute a chest for a sideboard.*

▓ *Start with a lamp to compose a table or chest top group. Hang a mirror with an interesting frame slightly above the lamp to reflect light. Have one made from an old frame. Notice how the tabletop elements overlap to create a cohesive composition.*

▓ *Finish with creative touches. Small terra-cotta pots and a wicker basket with a blooming seasonal plant imbue this chest top with style.*

▓ ***DESIGNERTIP*** *Every room does indeed benefit from a touch of black. Upgrade any lamp with a sleek black shade and new finial.*

▓ *Short a chair? Add a go-with-anything wicker find from an import store. Dress it up with pillows, buttons, and blanket-stitched detailing. (See page 102 for pillow sewing ideas and techniques.)*

▓ *Save money and add style by hanging an oil painting unframed. Illuminate with a battery-powered picture lamp from a home-center store.*

▓ *Paint the wall below the chair rail in a rich accent color that replicates a shade in your artwork.*

▓ *Jazz up a battered or unfinished desk with a crackled paint finish (see page 106) and new hardware. Add a table fan for a lighthearted and hot-weather-practical accent.*

▓ *Make easy-care draperies from paisley sheets. For easy how-to directions, see page 102.*

6-14

15-24

■ Stack vintage suitcases from your attic or a flea market on a sturdy wicker hamper, top left, for an instant bedside table and extra storage, too.

■ If your lamp still seems too low, elevate with books to achieve a comfortable reading height.

■ Bring the outdoors in with a garden-style bench for the foot of your bed. Add a cushion for extra seating. (If you have wood floors, make sure the metal feet are on felt so they don't scratch.)

■ Choose accessories that work with your color scheme. The wicker and twig doll chairs, left, and crackled-finish picture frames vary the textures without jolts of strong color. (For directions for the invitation board, see page 101; for crackled finish how-tos see page 106.)

■ Update an old dresser or chest with a pale antique finish. Detail with handpainted or stenciled stars, above. (See page 103 for how-tos.) Pair with a reproduction gilt-framed mirror hung above.

■ Nail in decorative upholstery tacks around the top, as shown, for the fashionable effect of nail heads.

■ Group, mat, and frame pairs of small prints, greeting cards, or even postcards for instant art.

■ Take your style one step beyond. Hang one framed pair of prints; lean the other for casual chic.

■ Create a conversation area with a pair of wicker chairs enlivened with accent pillows.

■ **DESIGNER TIP** Hang unlined burlap fabric as light-filtering, textured window treatments. Use iron rods and finials as decorative elements.

REFRESH YOUR FINDS WITH COLOR

25-30

Flea markets, thrift stores, and garage sales yield rich rewards for the diligent shopper. For not a lot of money, you can find pieces that add character to your room. The decorating challenge and fun is how to pull all your treasures together into a unified scheme. In the home shown here and on pages 16 and 17, classic blue and white, warmed by yellow, provide the key. When you have a lot of disparate elements, it does work best to limit and repeat your colors. For coziness without clutter, rotate your finds and use fewer, but larger decorative accents.

■ *Flank a display shelf with salvaged shutters for an instant grouping. Leave the shutters as is; rusting hinges and peeling paint contribute to the charm.*

■ *Revive a dated, but sturdy sofa with a slipcover in a scheme-setting pattern. If you sew, commercial patterns are available, or ask at a fabric store for names of seamstresses in your area. Choose a sturdy, washable cotton and put the slipcover on when it's slightly damp to avoid wrinkles.*

■ *Mix fabrics, patterns, trims, sizes, and shapes to have the most fun with pillows. Combine two or more fabrics into a stylish pillow top that takes advantage of leftover fabrics. (See page 102 for techniques and tips.)*

■ *Refresh old pieces with white paint. Here both the coffee table and side table were cleaned, lightly sanded, and painted with enamel. When the new paint is dry, lightly distress with sandpaper for a fashionably vintage look.*

■ *Emulate the look of paneling with molding strips, nailed in place with finishing nails. Paint the strips first, then measure and mark the wall. Touch up with paint. If you don't have a miter box, have a lumberyard cut the ends to fit.*

■ *Take advantage of out-of-the-ordinary display space to keep breakables safely out of reach. The space under a coffee table is best left to the sturdy, such as the dough bowl filled with balls of yarn.*

31-42

■ For instant impact, paint and paper a room in two colors. Choose one neutral as the supporting player to your focal-point color. White trim gives crisp contrast. Follow the natural breaks in the room, such as the ceiling-height change, opposite, created by the placement of the bay window.

■ For quick detailing, apply an architectural wallpaper border above, or in place of, a chair rail.

■ Break up a matched set for quick style. Here the old breakfast chairs mix with a contemporary glass table from an import store; the sturdy breakfast table found a home in the family room. Tie-on slipcovers give the chairs a softer look.

■ Make your own padded headboard, right, from cotton-print fabric, batting, and plywood. (See page 104 for how-tos.) For a unified look, repeat the headboard fabric in your window treatment.

■ Dress up pillow shams with buttons and trims. Or, buy a variety of pillows, such as king and queen sizes and European squares (26 inches square) and substitute for a conventional headboard.

■ For easy art with style and dimension, hang three metal postboxes (available from gift stores and catalogs) over your headboard and fill with dried flowers.

■ **DESIGNER TIP** Odd numbers of objects are more interesting than even in groupings.

■ In a small bedroom, take advantage of every bit of space. Use a small chest or even a wooden filing cabinet as a bedside table.

■ A candlestick-style lamp works well in these cramped quarters. If you have an odd candlestick, have a lamp shop turn it into a stylish lamp.

■ For instant luxury, dress a bed in two bed skirts, one slightly longer than the other.

■ Introduce a theme into your setting. The delicate cup and saucer, from the owner's collection, repeats the motif of the framed print, above. Or add a quirky piece from your flea market finds. The mannequin and hats give playful character.

■ Find a home for the odd chair or extra dining chair for putting on shoes. When space is tight, you have another surface for books and magazines.

INTRODUCE TEXTURES

Put away your paint chips. Don't get out the roller. Instead, turn to these quick-and-stylish ways to mix textures and add visual excitement to neutral walls and carpet. Think about what you have and what you need to pull the scheme together. Keep your main pieces—sofa, dining chairs, and dining table—simple and neutral. Let the easy-to-add and easy-to-change supporting players be the fun accents. For this look to work, mix the rough with the smooth, the rugged with the refined.

■ Mix things up. Combine the classic wood dining chairs (Chippendale style), opposite, a glass-topped table, and upholstered host and hostess chairs.

■ Fill in with a fun and fanciful painted screen—or make your own from hinged shutters or painted plywood cut to fit. (See page 106.)

■ Introduce a skirted table for softness and fabric in contrast to leggy furniture pieces. When this piece of particle board is topped with fabrics and glass,

it's welcome in any setting. (For details on making the skirts, see page 100.)

■ Stagger pairs of prints, above, flanking a large floral, to keep the eye moving. The pairs of prints are in the same style and mood for harmony.

■ Collect odd candlesticks in the same material and group them together on a coffee table.

■ Look for chairs that enhance your scheme with different textures, not match the sofa.

49-55

■ Think of bed posts as frames. Hang a traditional pair of matted prints between posts to take advantage of the symmetry.

■ Add a padded reproduction or antique bench at the foot of your bed. It's great for books and for stacking decorative pillows at night.

■ Show off a handsome vintage or new bed and dress it simply with only a tailored duvet. Here the toggle-style, sewn-on buttons add extra detailing to the large-scale plaid lining.

■ Use accent pillows to add pattern and texture without the distraction of bright color.

■ French-style scenic prints, called toile de Jouy, are ideal accent fabrics as they are typically one color on a white or off-white background. (See pillows opposite.) Mix with textured weaves and patterns.

■ **DESIGNER TIP** If storage isn't an issue and the doors are finished on both sides, open an armoire, wardrobe, or linen press to display a favorite collection. (Depending on how they are hinged, the doors may have to be removed and reversed to remain open as shown.) Employ the top for display.

■ Dress up wall-to-wall carpet with a small Oriental rug for pattern and color.

MAKE YOUR MASTER RETREAT

Comfort, calm, and style make a master retreat. For nonfussy good looks, start yours with an almost-instant headboard from a pair of old doors—or a large door hung horizontally is an equally handsome look. (Shutters are another alternative.) Look through salvage yards, thrift and junk shops, and flea markets for doors and shutters. Whatever you find and choose, simply clean and brush off loose paint and rust, as age is part of the charm. For comfort and more style, add large, firm pillows as your backrest. You'll need two to three on each side of the bed for enough support for easy reading.

▧ *Detail your "doors" with a pretty garland of dried flowers. (See page 105 for the how-to technique.)*

▧ *For extra storage, substitute two lightweight wicker hampers for a bedside table. The larger hamper is the perfect size for extra blankets and pillows, and the smaller hamper keeps bedtime reading handy but organized.*

▧ *Frame a section of a European damask tea towel for instant and stylish art. Choose a mat color to add vibrancy to the framed piece.*

▧ *Be creative with such accessories as this French metal flower container (or a wine bucket) for a different vase.*

▧ *Create your own vintage dressing mirror from an old frame. Or, age a new frame by darkening with artist acrylic paints in shades such as burnt umber or sienna.*

▧ *Loosen your look by leaning, rather than hanging, a print. The casualness is part of the charm.*

▧ *Use a plate rack to hold small hand towels, soaps, and sponges in your bath. A chair or a small stool is a nice touch of luxury, too.*

56-62

CREATE A PALETTE FOR CHANGE

For some of us, decorating isn't a project to be completed. Our homes are works in progress, and our interiors are ever-changing with the seasons, our newly acquired treasures, and even our current passions and moods. If you like the idea of quick-and-stylish change, keep the backdrop soft and neutral. And, restrict your rugs, window treatments, upholstered pieces, and even lamps to the equally unassuming. When art and objects and flowers of the season are the mainstays of your style, avoid the distraction of competing colors and patterns. Instead, introduce fabrics as accents that change, too, with the style of the moment. The idea is to cycle your favored pieces, not layer on, so have safe places to store your accessories and art until they are again in the limelight.

63–69

■ Bring the patio table from the porch or deck and have a ¹/₂-inch-thick glass round cut to size or check out ready-cut glass tops at import stores. If the style allows, use the base to store books.

■ Create table-top interest by elevating your lamp and an object or two on stacks of books. Vary the heights of objects for an interesting arrangement.

■ Think beyond the conventional for art. Here a handmade-paper card is displayed on a wrought-iron plate stand.

■ Minimize the distraction of colorful paintings with mirrors that reflect light and views of the outdoors. Look for frames that add instant detailing.

■ For most impact, group, don't scatter, your collections—such as the figures from Mexico on the carved chest.

■ "Slipcover" an ottoman with a woven knitted throw.

■ Rescue old furniture, such as these 1950s upholstered pieces, with simple, washable cotton-blend slipcovers. Add a decorative pillow in a compatible shape for a punch of color.

70-74

◼ Save a broken vase or bowl and display it as an art object in its own right. The bird's nest, found empty and out of season, holds tiny marble eggs.

◼ Rearrange your fireplace grouping and over-the-mantel art for a quick change of mood and seasons. For cooler months, enjoy cozy leather and fabric chairs. When you aren't building a fire, fill the firebox with decorative birch logs.

◼ Add a torchére floor lamp that bounces light off the ceiling, for a stylish accent that gives diffused nighttime lighting. Balance with an equally sleek tabletop lamp.

◼ During the heat of the summer, turn your back—and sofa—to the fireplace. Lean a trio of matching mirrors and small photographs in wide white mats for a cool-down look.

◼ Go asymmetrical by hanging small, framed artwork between the mantel and the window. Leave the other side bare.

75-
79

■ Go with the luxury of yardage, not costly fabric. Hang unlined, light-diffusing cotton from wrought-iron S-hooks. Rubber O-rings creatively and softly gather the fabric. (See page 105 for how-to instructions, including how to estimate the amount of fabric you'll need.) Notice how the draperies hang just under the simple crown molding and puddle gently on the floor for a graceful effect. When two rooms are open to each other, repeat the window treatment to avoid distraction.

■ Turn a blank corner into a still life worthy of a French Impressionistic painter. Fill your favorite large vase or pitcher with garden or wild flowers or branches and elevate on a plant stand. In the winter, even bare branches can be lovely in such a setting. Or try budding branches in early spring.

■ **DESIGNER TIP** Use a metal frog or wet florist foam and marbles to make sure your creation doesn't tip over.

■ If you like fabric accents, convert a yard or two into a runner that imparts color and style to a plain upholstered piece .

■ Balance elements. Here the visual weight of the dark mirror frame is repeated by the black lampshade.

WHEN YOU HAVE A FREE DAY TO DECORATE, TAKE advantage of the luxury of time with the room-by-room plans in this chapter. You'll find ideas to make the most of what you own and suggestions about versatile pieces and accessories to purchase. You'll also see ways to decorate with collections and projects to create baths, kids' rooms, or guest retreats. To get started, survey your room, decide what you can use and what you need. Before you shop, walk through your own home. You may have just the right piece of furniture or accessory that would star in a new setting. Designers suggest emptying a room and starting with a blank slate. Or even easier, remove everything except major furniture and window treatments.

THE DIFFERENCE A DAY MAKES

Moved from the dining room, this antique American secretary gives instant impact to a small foyer. A collection of Zulu baskets from Africa mix with pottery and books. On the practical side, the fine old piece adds a perfect place to drop keys and organize mail.

Living Rooms

Dining Rooms

Kitchens and Nooks

Master Bedrooms

Kids' Bedrooms

Family Rooms

Guest Rooms

PULLED TOGETHER
FOR LIVING

A

◼ **A** *Think beyond the "tired and true." Pair a leather sofa with a glass-topped table and sleek contemporary chairs for fireside dining. Note the angled furniture arrangement, too, for instant drama.*

◼ *For a side table with style, use an oversize plate rack for serving and display. Here the rack holds elongated fish platters.*

◼ *Lean unframed contemporary art on a mantel for a casual approach to high style. Place a pair of tall candlesticks asymmetrically.*

◼ *Warm a contemporary setting with folk or ethnic art, such as this ladder. Dark wood stands out against white walls.*

◼ *Use shelves to mix your collections with books. Employ the books to elevate objects and consider the dust jackets another way to add color.*

How many ways can you decorate an open living and dining room with a fireplace and built-in bookcases at one end and a pair of windows at the other? Here, and on the next two pages, we decorated the same spaces three different ways. If you like the idea of such an easy-to-change setting, keep the walls and flooring as neutral as you can—we used white walls and woodwork and natural oak floors. And, look for major furniture pieces, such as the glass-topped dining table and white sofa and chair, that work with a variety of styles and accessories. (Use washable white-cotton slipcovers as a durable, easy-care alternative to white upholstery.) For a different feel, switch the living and dining areas as we show here. In cooler months, nothing is more enjoyable than fireside dining, *below left*. And when you incorporate comfortable seating, your dining area doubles as the library. Notice, too, that what makes these rooms come alive is books and collected art. When you live with your passions, you create a warm, inviting home.

▦ **B** *Lean a mirror vertically to counterbalance the strong horizontal lines of the mantel. The flanking topiaries on wire stands and art-glass candlesticks give casual symmetry to the setting.*

▦ *Add another surface for informal dining and games with a large coffee table. Such a sturdy piece would be at home in a family room, too.*

▦ *Choose a classic white sofa and chair for the maximum in versatility. A throw and collections of pillows add color and pattern. Vary pillow sizes, textures, and trim but keep to the same degree of formality.*

▦ *Buy lightweight accent chairs in pairs for extra, easy-to-move seating. A pair of chairs instantly creates a versatile conversation area and can be moved around the room as needed.*

▦ **C** *Inject an elegant tone into your room and substitute a classic tea table for the conventional coffee table. A glass urn filled with fruit is equally chic. Or, use as a library table stacked with books.*

▦ *Get more impact from a small rug by angling it over sisal. In warm months, use the sisal alone for a cooled-down look.*

▦ *Employ the creative tension of unbalance by leaning a contemporary or classic painting at the side of your mantel and adding a striking piece of ethnic or folk art for the third, smaller element, such as the bowl.*

▦ *Stretch your decorating dollars with a pair of budget-priced, classic lamps, such as these gooseneck table lamps from a catalog.*

Set aside a day and turn your basic dining room or sitting room into a showcase for your own personal style. Here, with the same glass-topped table with metal base as on page 32, the dining room illustrates two very different looks from the traditional with a twist or two, center, to an eclectic blend of the classic, rugged, and arty. For another twist, the same space works equally well as the backdrop for a sitting area that's comfortable, *lower left*, but with a definite design edge. Note the impact of one large piece of art, rather than a grouping, and bright jolts of accent colors in otherwise neutral schemes. For a budget-stretcher, visit student art shows for large, bold canvases or mat and frame a museum exhibit poster.

A

93–104

▓ **A** *Stretch your budget by mixing large and small pillows. Three large pillows are the backdrop for a trio of small silk pillows.*
▓ *Drape unlined silk sheers over an iron rod and pin to the side. The look is casually elegant, the price is affordable, the time is minimal.*
▓ *Fill a blank hole in your decor with one large plant, which gives a room impact that can be lacking in a collection of small plants. Make sure you have sufficient sun and light.*
▓ *Mix contemporary, art-type furniture pieces or arty reproductions with vintage finds. Note a one-of-kind painted side table and an Eastlake-style side table from the turn of the century are in the same scale and balance as the low coffee table on wheels.*

KEY TO EASY STYLE ▦ *What can you accomplish in just a day? To make it easy and fun, consider your room as a canvas where anything goes. Start with rearranging major furniture pieces you plan to use. If it helps, measure and place pieces first on graph paper to get an idea of what could go where. Or, pull furniture away from the walls or angle pieces. Lighting makes a major difference so be open to the possibility of adding a lamp or two as you regroup. Candlestick lamps on the mantel or a small lamp or two in a built-in bookcase are possibilities. Try easy window treatments, such as the examples below, or experiment with different ways to use basic sisal carpeting and small rugs. And, remember that colorful new throw and accent pillows create instant impact.*

*▦ **B** No window treatments yet? No problem. These are simply draped and knotted from imported sari cloth from India. Measure the width and length you want to cover and then double it to make sure you have sufficient fabric. If you like a fuller look, triple the fabric. Alternative: Use any sheer fabric in a vibrant color and basic iron rods and finials.*

▦ When you have a special piece, such as this secretary or an armoire or cupboard, show its face by angling it into your room arrangement.

▦ Order fresh-flower topiaries, such as these roses, that dry into a permanent arrangement. The fading colors will add to the charm.

▦ Cover chair seats in a lighthearted plaid to relax formality. Remove the seats, stretch fabric over the forms, and staple in place.

*▦ **C** Loosen the formality of fixed velvet window treatment panels by hanging import-store bamboo shades behind for privacy and light control. The shades will help prevent fading and sun damage. Trim the velvet, draped over finial-style tiebacks, with large tassels.*

▦ Dine in eclectic style by pairing a refined bench with cushion and pillows and a rustic bench with the contemporary glass dining table. Arrange on an import-store sisal rug for the ultimate personal look.

▦ Fill large baskets with ornamental grass for style and no care.

▦ Pair a traditional, framed painting or print with folk art (the African piece on the stand). Or, for height, display an aged urn or vase on a pedestal or decorative plant stand.

DESIGN FOR LIVING

Scour your collections to pull together a living room fast. If you find you have a blank corner or two, so much the better—another excuse to visit your favorite flea market or shop. Start with a pretty background color and comfortable upholstery and let your collections do the rest. If you are thinking of painting your living room or re-covering an upholstered piece, use your collections to set the color palette. Take a tip from museums and rotate your finds every few months. You'll be rewarded with warmth and comfort, not clutter.

▓ *For this cottage look, collect architectural fragments from flea markets and thrift shops. Architectural salvage companies are other sources for these popular artifacts.*
▓ *Think beyond the obvious. Porch posts and balusters, below, double as pedestals.*
▓ *Shutters, opposite, are the perfect backdrops for art. Distress new ones if you can't find old.*
▓ *Be creative with quilts. Use a large, durable quilt to instantly "slipcover" a less-than-ideal sofa, below, as well as the always-popular hanging.*
▓ *Tape off and paint a checkerboard pattern on your fireplace surround and hang a favorite tray for a pretty finishing touch.*

105-109

110-116

Start with a neutral sofa and chair to transform a living room with sophisticated ethnic accents. If your upholstered pieces are busy florals or patterns, give them a quick fix with a canvas cloth slipcover. (See page 94 for how-to details.) Plain, contemporary-style lamps, such as the pharmacy lamp shown here, work well in the setting. Or, have a lamp made from an urn, jar, or African or Native American basket and finish with a natural or black shade. You'll have a relaxed retreat with the ambience of adventure.

DESIGNER TIP Use some larger pillows, at least 20 inches square, to anchor your arrangement. Earthy colors, such as rusts and brown, are good choices. Arrange pillows in batik, faux animal skin, or interesting scenic prints. Vary size, shape, and texture for the most interesting look.

Sisal or seagrass rugs add texture to hard-surface floors. If you have time and inclination, stencil details in an abstract pattern. If your floors are carpeted, use a small, abstract-pattern kilim or dhurrie rug.

Create one focal-point wall by tacking and draping cotton fabric at ceiling height. You'll need to measure your wall and double the fabric for a soft drape. Seam fabric and tack in place below the ceiling. Hang art through the cloth, as shown.

The point of ethnic decorating is the contrast of the dark and light, the rugged and the refined. Keep small accessories to a minimum and go with larger pieces that add texture, such as this mask on a stand.

When you have small objects, group them together. Note how the decorative balls fill the dough bowl elevated to prominence on a rustic iron stand.

Choose your plants and containers carefully. One large plant gives much more impact than a collection of small houseplants. Add an orchid in a clay or hammered metal pot for a special finishing touch.

DESIGN
FOR DINING

Style, warmth, and welcome, not costly furnishings, are the true measures of a dining room. With today's very personal decorating, work with what you have and what you like. The bonus is that you mix pieces and add to a room over time to create just the look that fits your style and budget. When you employ versatile furnishings, they easily can move from your dining room to a breakfast nook or even to a bedroom or family room as your mood and style evolve.

▧ Hang a quilt, below, at the ceiling molding. Avoid exposure to direct light and rotate with other quilts to avoid excessive wear.

▧ Use a dry sink for serving and holding napkins and placemats. Other sideboard alternatives: dropleaf table, butler's tray on stand, vintage or reproduction chest, or large painted metal tray on a serving stand.

▧ **DESIGNER TIP** When you are shopping for a dining table, a round table with a leaf is particularly versatile, as it works in a smaller space and expands for guests.

▧ Flowers fade after your dinner party or brunch. Buy a trio of herb topiaries in clay pots. Elevate on white flea-market plates that protect your table or server.

▧ A farm table, right, imparts a sturdy charm to a

dining room. For a relaxed look, leave the top stained and paint and distress the base and legs.

▧ Need extra seating? Use wing chairs for host and hostess chairs that add fabric and pattern. Consider shapes as wings repeat curves of the more formal chairs.

▧ For long-lasting table arrangement, place ivy topiaries in glazed pottery jars. Add fresh roses for parties.

▧ Turn your dining area, opposite, into library dining with a narrow table that doubles for writing.

▧ Create an easy-to-change gallery library by leaning framed photographs or prints against the wall and use open storage for books.

117-125

CREATE KITCHEN CHARM

No longer merely utilitarian, kitchens today are filled with charm and personality and savvy decorating ideas. If yours is lacking sparkle, think how you can incorporate what you do and what you like, your passions, into the design. Here, the answer is obviously shopping and gift bags—many, many shopping bags, which are easy to find and eminently fun and colorful. Other ideas: collections of vintage or new pottery or glassware (stick to one type or color family for most dramatic effect), pitchers, teapots, baskets, cookie jars, antique kitchen tools or toys, miniature tables and chairs, even your own children's or grandchildren's artworks. Start with a clean slate, such as the freshly painted cabinets here, and keep fabric and other distractions to a minimum.

▓ *Fill the blank, boring space between your cabinets and the ceiling with your favored collectibles. They don't have to be valuable, just fun. Stay with one type of object—from these colorful shopping and gift bags to pottery bowls to Native American baskets— to avoid a hodgepodge of disparate elements. Just make sure what you group and display is large enough to be seen and appreciated from below.*

▓ *If you have the counter space, borrow a little for your collection, but be careful to avoid clutter. Vary the shapes and sizes for interest.*

▓ *Passionate collectors quickly run out of room. Look for creative venues for display, such as the ledge over the windows in the breakfast nook.*

▓ *Where light control and privacy aren't considerations, hang tiny bags, via S-hooks, from a tension rod.*

▓ *If you need more privacy and like this idea, use cafe curtains or shutters on the lower panes. Or, tuck in a roller shade or blinds.*

126-130

BEDROOM BASICS

Spend today redecorating and you can spend tonight in your own personal retreat. Who doesn't need a comfortable place to unwind from the cares of the world? If your bedroom is already painted in a favorite soothing color or a neutral you can live with, you have a head start. If not, make this a two-day project and choose your favorite calm-down color, such as a pretty shade of blue, green, or lavender, for paint. If you are unsure of the exact shade you want, pick out a color from the fabric you are using or plan to use in the room.

▨ *Choose the fabric that will set the tone you want. To emulate the romantic cottage bedroom here, look for a gently scaled floral in soft pastels. Use this fabric for the window treatment and at least two other accents.*

▨ *In a hurry? Many pretty ready-made window treatments that coordinate with comforters and sheets are now available. Shop department stores and home furnishing stores for a quick-start on your bedroom. Personalize these basics with pillow shams, pillows, and throws you mix in. If you have time, make an assortment of pillows from fabric scraps and trims. (See page 102 for how-tos.)*

▨ ***DESIGNER TIP*** *For comfort and lush style, you'll need six regular bed pillows sized for a double-, queen-, or king-size bed. Dress the back two pillow in shams, and the other four in two pillowcases each.*

▨ *As an alternative, buy two European square pillows (26 inches square) and four regular pillows. Many types of pillows—from down to various hypoallergenic stuffings—are sold at a variety of prices and degrees of firmness.*

▨ *Consider other pillow shapes that work well in the bedroom, such as the neckroll (6 x 14 inches) and boudoir (12 x 16 inches).*

▨ *For today's mix and match styles, make up your bed in layers. A bedspread alone can look bleak so add a quilt or throws or both. In summer, use a cotton coverlet with a light throw. In winter, dress your*

bed in flannel sheets and a duvet or comforter. Add extra quilts and throws for cocooning warmth.

▨ *Every bedroom needs a comfortable spot for sitting and relaxing. Arrange a chair for reading and a table for a snack and tea. If space is tight, use a plant stand for a small drink table.*

▨ *Make sure you have vision-friendly light for reading. Swing-arm lamps, with three-way switches, are ideal as they adjust easily.*

131-138

148-152

■ Decorate a bath with leaf-motif stamps you purchase in desired shapes or make yourself. (For instructions on making your own leaf stamps from real leaves, see page 107.) Here's how to create the subtle, elegant stamped projects shown here:

■ For walls, stamp a row of leaves at natural breaks in the room, such as above the sink as shown here. Along the ceiling and around trims and windows are other natural locations. Select from a variety of paints, as flat latex paints, glazes, and acrylics all work well. Use muted colors for a seasonless look.

■ For canvas stamping, wash medium-weight canvas in warm water and dry. Custom-make a curtain or skirt in the size you need. Stamp the leaf design around the edges with acrylic-based fabric paints.

■ For hand towels, use a tightly woven natural fabric, such as cotton or linen. Machine wash and dry. Don't use fabric softeners. Press and tape down. Stamp with acrylic-based fabric paints.

■ For rugs, use a natural fabric and flatly woven surface, not a nap, and fabric paint.

BRIGHTEN KIDS' ROOMS

Has someone in your family outgrown his or her room? Do you suddenly have a teenager in residence? Choose a Saturday that's good for you both and get to work. It's surprising what four hands can accomplish in a day. Because color gives the most bang for the decorating buck, it's a good place to start. Decide beforehand if color change is coming and have the supplies ready. A gallon of paint will be enough to transform an average-size bedroom. And you just might have a willing painter in your midst.

▓ *Go sophisticated with teen color. In the bedroom,* opposite, *two cans of paint—dramatic cobalt blue and white—totally changed a dull room.*

▓ *Note here that linens, rug, and accessories stay within the color palette boundaries. Lavish use of white keeps blue from overpowering.*

▓ *For a softer look, consider a paler shade of blue. Or, add yellow or yellow-and-white accents.*

▓ *Employ finishing touches. Freshly painted white, the reproduction metal stars glow against the dark blue wall. Use shelves to display treasures, awards, and winning ribbons.*

▓ *Have some fun. The drawer fronts* right, *below the built-in beds, sport decoupaged sections of road maps. Trim and knobs are painted with gloss enamel. (See page 108 for details.)*

▓ *Frame old 45 rpm records.*

153-162

Or, frame one old record album or a pair of vintage albums.

▓ *Utilize a wide window ledge and lean a framed print against the window.*

▓ *Take an easy out and have a uniform shop stitch your child's name on an oversize pillow top.*

▓ *Stitch a spread fitted to a bunk bed. (See page 108.)*

▓ *Craft a playful bed,* left, *for your fan. (See page 109 for instructions.) Choose the scheme in favorite team colors (here the red, white, and blue of the Atlanta Braves). Dress the bed in appropriately sturdy pillows and linens.*

LIGHTEN UP
A PLAYROOM

In a room where play is the purpose, take a lighthearted approach to decorating. The room featured here is the haven of parents and teens alike and filled with reminders of their favorite hobbies and adventures. In a room for younger children, go with a sparer approach and keep the collections up and away. What works for all ages are the vinyl floor, spiffed up with randomly set colored vinyl tiles, and the big, comfy plaid sofa and pillows. Quilts and throws, too, are good for curling up together.

163-171

▓ Go light and bright with your color scheme. Or, try the camp look of greens and rusty browns.

▓ Wicker hampers make great, easy-to-move side and coffee tables. Use them to store games, books, bedding for the sofa bed, magazines, and clutter.

▓ Create an instant wall grouping by organizing your finds with a screen-door frame—the more decorative the shape, the better. This one was red. If yours is dull, paint it to contrast with the wall.

▓ The more battered the better when it comes to furniture. Find an old storage cabinet and simply clean and brush off the loose paint.

▓ *DESIGNERTIP* Have a table lamp made from a favorite figure or object, such as the Texas steer shown here. Or, choose a funky vase or aged urn.

▓ Recycle a damaged quilt by salvaging pieces to recover a wing chair or other comfortable chair. Use smaller scraps for a footstool, ottoman, or pillows.

▓ Incorporate your hobbies into the scheme. Here the creel basket and rods and old trophies add to the fishing memorabilia.

▓ Look for the unusual. A copper pot with handles gives dimension to the wall. The stained-glass window diffuses and colors afternoon sunlight.

▓ Expand your sources. The bears and canoe here came from an outdoor outfitting store.

INSTANT GUEST ROOM

You heard the wake-up call. Company is coming, and your guest room is bare. Or worse, it has evolved into the dreaded spare room (also known as junk room). With that call to arms, it's time to get busy. Clear the decks by adding storage boxes under the bed or donating never-used items to charity. Then concentrate on creating an inviting space. Make the bed with a padded mattress pad or feather bed over the mattress for extra softness. Buy all-cotton sheets and wash and iron them. Make sure you have at least three pillows for a single bed, six for a double. Lightly starch pillowcases before ironing. Use two top sheets with a light blanket between for extra comfort. Depending on your climate and the season, top the bed with a duvet, comforter, or light coverlet. By the bedside, place a small table, good reading lamp, alarm clock, and fresh flowers. A double bed needs a table and lamp on each side. Don't worry about them matching; it's more charming if they don't.

■ *No headboard for your bed frame? Tie branches, opposite, together for true twig furniture. Attach it to the wall with hooks, rather than to the bed frame. (For other headboard ideas, see pages 104—105.)*

■ *Dress up a ready-made window mirror, above, with cup hooks to hang straw hats and a dried flower garland. (For more on attaching a dried garland, see page 110.)*

■ *No window treatments yet? Add simple, tie-on ones, left. (For other ideas on quickly making your own, see pages 102 and 105.) Install stock blinds or shades for instant privacy and light control.*

■ *In a small room, angle the bed to avoid a boxy look and feel. When space is tight, use one table by the bed and the other in front of the window.*

■ *Arrange a wicker hamper and basket at the foot of the bed. Use the hamper for extra pillows and blankets. Fill the basket with new magazines.*

■ *Also nice for a guest room are a carafe and water glass, tissues, clock radio, and padded coat hangers.*

TAKE ADVANTAGE OF A FREE AFTERNOON to rearrange your furniture and organize favorite collections or accessories. Just moving a piece or two gives a room a whole new look and feel. Consider what you want to display and where and how to show your favorites to the fullest effect. If you need a find or two to fill out your grouping, it's fine to mix reproduction with vintage collectibles, heirlooms with flea-market finds. Start by experimenting with an easy-to-change tabletop and simple wall grouping. Coffee tables are an ideal beginning just as elevating an accessory or adding a plant creates instant drama. If you are shopping for a coffee table, consider a glass top to allow rugs or objects below to show through.

Living Rooms

Dining Rooms

Mantels and Fireplaces

Shelves and Bookcases

Tabletops

Displays for Art, Objects,

and Family Heirlooms

AFTERNOON
ARRANGEMENT

Use a small stand for dramatic tabletop display. Even when you group like objects, vary the heights for interest. As an alternative, stack magazines or art books to raise a bowl, vase, or urn.

THE WELL-ARRANGED ROOM

For a welcoming living room, place furniture and accessories to work together. To create this comfortable environment, pull furniture toward the center of the room, away from the walls. Cluster chairs close enough for easy conversation and make sure every chair has a table nearby that's handy for drinks or books. If you occasionally need extra seating, place easy-to-move accent chairs in corners so they can be pulled in when needed. Add what you like to see every day and what makes you feel good.

■ *Take advantage of the architecture of your stairs. Here the exposed stairway wall becomes a gallery for display. And, the landing adds the perfect spot to show off an unframed oil painting, casually elevated on stacked hampers.*

■ *Create convivial sitting areas by pairing chairs and arranging so they share a side or coffee table. In a room without a foyer, place major pieces at right angles to the front door and turned into the room to give the illusion of an entry hall.*

■ *Hang a handsomely framed vintage portrait or photograph in a prominent place of honor. If you don't have an inherited one, look through flea markets for old photographs or oils. Also shop for small occasional or accent tables made from the turn of the century through the 1920s and often sold at bargain prices in secondhand stores. Don't worry about refinishing; the aged look contributes to the charm and style.*

■ *Add a sconce to a grouping of small pictures. If you need a real light source, have it electrified; if not, a candle sconce is an economical and fashionable alternative. Group frames of different shapes and materials for a casual arrangement.*

■ *Use large baskets, such at this split-oak basket, for storage and quick accents. Look for such regional baskets as you travel or check out handmade baskets at craft fairs.*

178-182

A TOUCH OF COUNTRY

Refine a room by carefully editing furniture and accessories. Fewer, larger pieces—an armoire or a cupboard and pair of tables—instantly impart more drama than several smaller ones. If your favorite pieces seem to be getting lost in the shuffle of treasures and collections, think about the pieces you need and the accessories you want to spotlight. See how the room looks and works with one less chair or table. Or, replace a busy wall grouping with one large, handsomely framed mirror or painting.

▧ *Simplify a setting by replacing a picture or grouping with a framed mirror, opposite. The mirror reflects light without adding color to a neutral decorating scheme.*

▧ *Cut down table clutter. Display three to five interesting pieces (depending on your table or desk size) rather than a full collection.*

▧ **DESIGNER TIP** *Move up the scale. When you use fewer pieces, use larger ones to add impact interest without overload.*

▧ *Choose pieces that serve double duty. The writing desk, opposite, adds storage and also a tabletop for display and writing.*

▧ *Look for new uses for what you have. A plate rack, stored away for entertaining, works wonderfully as a plant stand. Collect flea-market plates for saucers. Stack books on the lower rung, if you prefer.*

▧ *Place a small cotton rug underneath the plate rack to keep the feet from scratching your floor. (If floor space is tight, use it on a chest or console table.)*

▧ *In a simplified setting, above, one great piece, such as a Victorian plant stand, sets the lively, not-too-serious tone.*

▧ *Keep accessories minimal, but interesting. Look for new or vintage birdcages for a lighthearted accessory.*

▧ *Add interest without patterned fabric by hanging a flea-market or antique-store stained-glass window to reflect colors.*

▧ *Frame a pair of botanical prints, from a calendar, in eye-catching heavy frames. Hang them close together so they work as one unified piece of art.*

Use your kitchen to display both fun and practical
accessories. A few key pieces go a long way in
creating a warm, welcoming space.

▦ Hang a country-style shelf for jars filled with dried
beans and pasta, right, and use the pegs below for
a pretty, decorative apron and straw hat.

▦ Measure three to six of your collected plates and
make a simple plate rack to fit, below. The length of
the rack depends on how much wall space you have.
Use molding strips for the rack and hang at the
corners with picture hangers and hooks.

▦ Dress up your range or cooktop with a colorful
platter or try a metal tray for a similar effect.

▦ Decorate with nature's bounty. Buy a wire basket
and pottery bowls for the fruits or vegetables of the
season. For a different effect, mix purple, yellow,
and white onions with potatoes.

▦ Collect old-fashioned, country-store candy and
cookie jars, below, and use them for canisters.

▦ Mix in baskets, opposite, to give a lighter look to
a pot rack—and to fill in while you finish collecting
pots. Pot racks are perfect, too, for strings
of garlic or dried peppers.

▦ Frame a fruit or vegetable print for your breakfast
nook wall. Or, look for a poster or calendar art that
has similar motifs. One larger piece keeps the look
clean and simple and is less busy than a grouping.
Hang a spice rack below as a decorative accent.

▦ Buy or stitch a simple, plain cotton runner for your
table. Use durable, washable fabric. Add a lace panel
or cutwork panel to your windows or door.

193-
200

GROUP YOUR COLLECTIBLES

223-233

■ *Give a dropleaf table a new purpose as a fashionable demilune (half-round) table, above left. This space-saver provides an interesting shape for a tabletop. Keep the look simple with a framed mirror. (If the mirror is large enough, lean rather than hang.)*

■ *It's fun to get a theme going. Here the star-motif picture frame repeats as the decorative papier-mâché star.*

■ **DESIGNERTIP** *Vary heights. Note the stand for the vase here, the small photograph on an easel, and the displayed books. But don't obscure elements. Notice how the tall candlestick is placed to the side.*

■ *Utilize the space under a leggy console table for extra storage and decorating, as the wicker hamper above illustrates. Other alternatives*

If you are a collector, you look for places to display your finds. Your mission is to organize and arrange your treasures for impact and enjoyment. But, even if you aren't seriously committed to pursuing a particular passion, you probably have the beginning of a collection that will add personality to your rooms. Walk around your home and look through cabinets, cupboards, and stored-away boxes (and even your children's rooms). Using what you have, fill in with flea-market and thrift-store pieces or reproductions. And see what fun it is to incorporate collections and memorabilia into your decorating. For easy organization and a focal point, think of your display space as a table or chest top and the wall above. The tabletop anchors the arrangement, creating visual strength. As a quick start, choose one major element, such as a print, pair of prints, or mirror, and work out from there. This avoids the distraction of a collection of only small objects.

include flat baskets to organize stacked magazines or large pots.

■ **DESIGNER TIP** To group such disparate elements as the wall arrangement, above, work out your placement first on the floor. Measure the space you have to work with and mark off the same area on your floor with a tape measure so you have an accurately sized surface.

■ Use an erasable pencil and tape measure or straightedge to mark where to hang your largest elements. Take into account the top of your table arrangement. Hang the center elements first, working bottom to top to see how the grouping looks.

■ Vary shapes, sizes, and frames for interest. The bulls-eye-style gilt mirror becomes important with the prints around it. When you flank a mirror

with prints, match the style and framing for pleasing continuity.

■ Stick to one type of collection. The majolica-style green plates have more punch than a mix of styles and patterns. Plate hangers, available in small to platter sizes, make display safe and easy.

■ Add snapshots or photographs, but don't overdo. Two or three have more impact than a crammed tabletop.

■ Look for something with dimension, rather than flat, such as these chairs, above right, to collect. The size mix adds to the appeal.

■ Go all the way. Include art (the prints) that amplifies your theme. When you have enough, restrict your grouping to one type of object or one theme. The chair prints are a playful focal point.

DISPLAY YOUR CREATIVITY

While you are either saving up for art or still looking for some fresh alternative approaches, consider the impact of groupings of frames or mirrors. The arrangements work because they group like objects with interesting detailing—variations on a definite theme. Artless frames are inventive and fun as they repeat one clever idea but vary the shapes and materials. Mixing framed art and empty frames, on the other hand, would be disconcerting as it would lack a decorating theme. Frames, without art, also work in bookcase arrangements, when hung inside shelves.

234-240

■ Stairwells are notoriously difficult to decorate because of the graduated spaces. A collection of small mirrors, in varying sizes, frames, and shapes, opposite, gently climbs the stairs and fills the wall.

■ Look at how the mirrors are stacked and ordered in vertical rows to follow the rise of the staircase.

■ Stairwells also are classic display walls for family photographs. For a clean look, have photographs identically matted and framed. New and old photographs take on a contemporary twist.

■ Flea markets and secondhand shops are the hunting grounds for old frames, above. (Don't hesitate to remove a painting or print.) If you are short of one or two, look at the sale bins in frame shops.

■ Age an ornate new frame with artist acrylics or sanding off some of the gilt paint and shine.

■ Odd numbers are more interesting than even. Two unmatched pairs flank the round frame, above.

■ Stagger your arrangement. Notice the uneven distances the frames are hung above the chair rail.

▨ Stack a collection of still life oil paintings, below left, *in a blank corner. The repetition of style and medium creates the composition.*

▨ *Hang paintings as unframed canvases to emulate the casual look of an art studio (and save on frames). Frame one piece as accent.*

▨ *Before hanging, group on the floor to create a composition that pleases you. Consider how you will fill the space—three smaller paintings, below left, balance two larger ones.*

▨ *When art is stacked, it's more pleasing if pieces are fairly close in size. A single, very small painting looks out of scale when stacked above or below a very large one.*

▨ *For a different and instant change of pace,* hang a print or watercolor from a window frame, below right.

▨ *Work out a grid for prints, opposite. Measure your wall space and arrange the framed prints in the same dimensions on the floor. Calculate how much space you need to leave between prints (at least the width of the frame). Leave the same amount of wall space on each side of each print for a neat grid.*

▨ ***DESIGNER TIP*** *Determine where to hang the center print, then measure and mark with a pencil. Hang the middle row first vertically, then work out from there.*

▨ *Maximize small prints by mounting in wide double mats with decorative frames.*

241-248

CREATE A FOCAL POINT

In a space without the natural focus of a fireplace or dramatic art, take advantage of the decorative possibilities of storage and display. For a subtle feel, paint the display shelf or shelves in the same color as your walls. Or for a bolder stroke, pick a lively contrasting color or rich wood stain. For built-ins, choose between the calm of blending with the wall and the design interest of choosing a richer color for the back wall. If shelves are white, for example, choose a dark red or rich chocolate brown as the backdrop for books and display pieces. Or, even simpler, paint the trim, as shown *below*, for just a touch of color.

249-254

▓ *Purchase a display shelf or make one from a plywood box trimmed with molding.*

▓ *Group like objects, such as the figures, opposite; don't overfill. If some are smaller than others, vary elevations with stands or stacks of decorative books.*

▓ *Respect your books, left. Arrange them without wedging. Paperbacks and magazines are fine, too. (They show you are a reader.) But they look neater when they are grouped together.*

▓ *Organize your family photos with matching, simple white mats and natural frames.*

▓ *Hang one unusual or more colorful frame or matted photograph. And, use an easel or two for variation in display.*

▓ *Add a lamp or shelf light for the warmth of light. And, soften hard edges with a basket brimming with baby's breath.*

DISPLAYING YOUR TREASURES

From the entry to the kitchen to your own bedroom, live with the collections you love. When you've already filled your mantel, tabletops, and living and dining room walls, look beyond the obvious for clever display. Think about ways to integrate favorite pieces throughout your home with ease. The foyer is a good choice as it gives the first impression for your home. Try a collection of plates over a foyer chest, as shown *below*, or if space is tight, even above a narrow table or bracket shelf. If you don't have a foyer, display collectibles on chest, table, shelf, or brackets that guests see when they open the door. Group less formal collectibles, such as baskets or pottery, on a bench by the back door.

255-260

■ When your cupboards are crowded with majolica (pottery with a translucent glaze), opposite, or other plates, create a bedside grouping with a swing-arm reading lamp.

■ There's no right or wrong way to decorate with plates. Some collectors group by type, pattern, material, or color.

■ Or, you may like to mix new and old, family heirlooms and flea-market finds. Remember that it's easier to get a pleasing look when you stick to one material, such as the delicate painted porcelain china plates, opposite.

■ Create balance with odd sizes and patterns by arranging them first on the floor to work out what you like. Work with a symmetrical grouping and vary it to accommodate odd numbers and different sizes.

■ If you collect commemorative plates, hang together and mix with other collections, above, for more color.

■ Add a kitchen cupboard, above, to display what you use every day. Notice how the goblets are turned upside down to show off the interesting stems and bases.

QUICK TIPS FOR COLLECTING

Want to make the most of what you love? Keep the backgrounds simple and noncompeting. The collections here stand out against the simplest of all backgrounds—flat-white walls and woodwork and glossy painted white floors. (Natural or pickled wood floors or neutral wall-to-wall carpet or sisal would work well, too.) When you decorate with collections and art, keep pattern and fabric to a minimum. Instead of fussy curtains or patterned draperies, consider the simple style of shutters, shades, or sheers. Lighting fixtures are supporting players. Recessed lighting and simple lamps are options to chandeliers.

■ *Choose one object with a strong, easy-to-read shape as your focal point. The large pitchers, below left, the trade-sign apple, below, and the cow silhouette, opposite, fill the bill.*

■ *Focus the grouping by centering the collectibles you want to spotlight. Shelves effectively organize a number of objects, opposite. Leave plenty of breathing room so your treasures aren't crowded by supporting players.*

■ *Group objects of similar visual weight and feel. Duplicate objects, such as the ceramic pumpkins and majolica pitchers, opposite, illustrate the familiar visual strength of arranging with strict symmetry.*

■ *For creating a pleasing tabletop arrangement, group rather than scatter. Even with carefully edited objects, employ the principle of overlapping triangles (see pitchers, left). Limit the number of like objects for a clean look.*

■ *Use a mix of textures, rather than a number of slick or polished objects, for a warm, friendly feel.*

■ *Treat folk art as contemporary art. Hang large pieces alone, below, rather than as part of a busy grouping.*

261-266

EVEN IF YOUR FREE TIME COMES IN INCREMENTS of minutes, not days, you can still enjoy the satisfying pleasures of decorating. With only a stolen hour or two, you can do more than you may think. Gather your supplies and tools first and you'll have a head start on quickly accomplishing your project. Try one quick touch for a room, such as a window treatment (shown here or on the next two pages) or no-sew slipcover for a battered sofa or fresh flowers in an interesting container. Add a touch or two more as you can and you'll soon fill your home with your own personal, creative decorating style. That, not time, is what decorating is all about.

Window Treatments

Skirted Tables

Furniture Finds

Instant Slipcover

Flowers in a Flash

AN HOUR
OR TWO...OR LESS

For a summer-fresh treatment, predrill seashells and tie to transparent white ribbons. To hang, slip ribbons over a tension rod and tie as single loops. Leave fluttery, long streamers. Hang 2 to 3 inches above the sill so the shells blow in the breeze.

WINDOW TRICKS
QUICK!

When you want to soften, not cover, turn to the magic of lacy sheers and translucent ribbons. You'll be able to find pretty ready-made curtains or sheer fabrics with finished edges and sides. Employ a tension rod or decorative tacks for the ultimate in no-hassle hanging. For a lush look, use two curtain panels for each average, double-hung window. Or, create delicate treatments with lengths of organza or other barely-there types of ribbons. Fabric and craft stores, and florist's supply shops, are sources for a variety of patterns and widths of ribbons by the yard.

■ *Hand-stitch ties, cut from ribbon, to ready-made sheer gauze panels,* opposite. *Tie ribbons into bows and loop over hooks spaced above the frame. (For bows, use 18 to 24 inches of ribbon.)*

■ *Casually drape a filmy white cloth at a summertime window,* above. *Hot-glue decorative stars to sturdy tacks and simply push into the wooden frame. Add a third star as a tieback.*

■ *Adapt the French idea of portierés (interior drapery panels used as a divider) for a ribbon treatment,* left. *Fasten a metal rod directly to the ceiling with wood screws. Attach ribbons to drapery rings and hang from rod. Use ribbons from the same color family.*

■ *For a cafe-style look, fold a voile or cutwork tablecloth over a rod; hang so the corners hang in off-centered points.*

■ *To emulate cafe curtains, clip vintage, embroidered pillowcases or tea or guest towels to a length of clothesline with wooden clothespins. Or, try large napkins or bandannas. Attach the line inside your window frame with a pair of screw eyes.*

SKIRTING THE COVER-UP DEBATE

A classic that's always stylish, a skirted table enhances just about any setting. The fashionable fabrics conceal what's underneath—economical, particleboard tables that are easy to assemble and available in discount and home furnishings stores and from decorating catalogs. Standard sizes include 24-inch diameter × 24-inch height; 30-inch diameter × 30-inch height; and 36-inch diameter × 30-inch height. To gracefully cover your table, you'll need a 72-inch-diameter round cloth for a 24-inch table; a 90-inch-diameter for a 30-inch table; and a 96-inch-diameter for a 36-inch table.

272-277

■ Use a vintage linen as an overlay and protect with a ¼-inch glass top, above. The glass also protects sentimental treasures, such as photographs, invitations, announcements, and pressed flowers.

■ As a variation on this theme, substitute snapshots from family vacations or special milestones, postcards, or prized sports cards.

■ Have a monogram shop make leaves from scrap fabric, right, and then appliqué to a purchased round cotton or cotton-blend cloth.

■ Want to use a square or rectangular cloth for the skirt? No problem. As long as length and width are slightly longer than the necessary diameter (see copy at top), it will work. Simply tuck under the edges.

■ For a small table, depending on your style, use a vintage lace doily, silk head scarf, monogrammed napkin, or bandanna for the topper.

■ Trimming ideas: Hot glue wide rickrack or other decorative trim 3 inches above the hem of a purchased cloth. Sew large buttons 6 inches apart and 3 inches from the hem and drape decorative cording between buttons. Or, stencil border with fabric paint. (See page 107.)

278–285

■ Tie a quilt with raffia over a purchased underskirt, opposite. Or, use a larger quilt as the skirt and a smaller round cloth overlay or combine two quilts. Protect with glass top.

■ As alternatives to quilts, use camp or Western-motif blankets or coverlets.

■ Emulate the tying technique, opposite, with alternative fabrics and ties. Pair damask cloths in two solid colors—or a solid with a print or plaid that echoes your scheme. Tie with cording, braid, or grosgrain ribbon.

■ Substitute the largest table round (36 inches in diameter) for a small dining table. Or, check out the sturdy (and storable) round tables from restaurant supply houses.

■ For convivial dinner parties too large for your dining table, store an extra round table or two and set up with director's or slipcovered folding chairs as needed.

■ Mix cloths of two different patterns for a lively look. Choose fabrics with a color in common, such as the stripes and abstract print, above. For a Country French look, combine a solid with a small print in a bright yellow, red, blue, or green.

■ Look for ready-made skirts with interesting details, such as cording, above. Specialty catalogs are sources for a wide range of table skirts and overlays.

■ Angle a square cloth as the overlay. The points create design interest as another element of the skirt. Swap the overlay for a quick change of season or mood. In winter, use a throw or lap blanket. In summer, try picnic-style tablecloths.

NEW ROLES
FOR OLD PIECES

Think beyond the obvious when it comes to furnishing your home with your personal stamp. There are no right and wrong ways to use tables or table substitutes. Any piece can go anywhere as long as it fits the scale and style of the room. If you don't need a table you originally bought for your living room, move it into your bedroom or guest room. Or, if you collect, consider ways to incorporate your finds into working members of your decor (note the wagon, *below right*).

■ *Go with what works. A set of gilded French Provincial-style nesting tables, below left, groups as a pretty bedside table.*

■ *Depending on the height of your bed and the space you have, a library ladder, bench, chest, even a small wrought iron or wood patio table works at bedside.*

■ *Vintage wood wagons are great finds. So, too, are the classic red metal ones—the more battered the better. Or, use your children's outgrown wagon in a playroom or family room. Fill with plants or cookbooks to brighten the kitchen.*

■ *Need a sturdy, put-up-your-feet coffee table? Cut down a farm table, opposite, and sand the legs smooth. Or, use a garden bench as an equally rugged alternative.*

■ *Elevate an import-store porcelain planter (sometimes called a Chinese fish bowl or jardiniere) or large terra-cotta pot on a sturdy stand and top with a glass round. Or, use two jardinieres with glass tops for dining.*

■ *For a writing table, pair a sawhorse or two wood filing cabinets with a painted or stained door or ³⁄₄-inch plywood plank or ½-inch glass top cut to fit.*

286-291

GIVE AN OUTDATED LOOK THE SLIP

Here's a temporary fix that's so stylish you just might make it a permanent solution. Instead of re-covering or even slipcovering an old sofa, conceal with an economical painter's canvas dropcloth (see the before and after photographs *below* and *opposite*). Instantly, you'll have a chic white sofa that will fit into any decor or setting. And because the dropcloth is generously sized (large sizes are 9×12 feet), you'll have plenty of fabric to tuck and drape to give an old piece a new, softer shape.

BEFORE

■ Buy the largest size drop cloth for an average sofa. You'll need the extra yardage to fold and pleat stamped writing out of sight and to tuck under seat cushions to hold the cloth in place. Use a smaller size, such as 8×10, for a loveseat or a large, upholstered chair.

■ Place the sofa legs over the drop cloth to help hold it snugly in place.

■ For a softer surface, wash the dropcloth in cold water and dry. You'll need to use a large commercial washing machine in a self-service laundry because of the bulk of the fabric.

■ White pillows (at least 20 inches square) and throws give sophisticated accents to your "new" sofa, or add pillows that enhance your decor. Change accents and colors with the seasons.

■ For a dressier look, buy a matelasse coverlet or spread made for a king-size bed. Or, for a country look, use a quilt-style spread made for a king-size bed.

292-296

CREATIVE DISPLAYS IN A FLASH

Hands down, flowers give you the quickest, easiest impact for your decorating dollar. For instant arrangements, keep a collection of clear glass vases, carafes, or jars on hand. Add a single stem of the same type of flower to each, and an arrangement is born. Or collect decorative olive oil, imported soda, wine, or water bottles. Besides clear glass, you'll be able to stock up on cobalt blue and pale green bottles. And, you'll find shapes from the tall, skinny, square bottles to short, rounded-bottom bottles with narrow necks.

■ *With a milk-bottle carrier and small carafes, you only need eight stems for a fresh, lively arrangement. Flowers with stiff stems, such as daisies, below left, are easiest to work with as they don't droop.*

■ *Transform a tiered pie-and-bread server, below, or a plate rack into a centerpiece for your table or sideboard. Add a bunch of small wildflowers at the top and balance with a trailing green plant.*

■ *Select a container with a small opening to hold tall flowers easily in place. For pleasing proportion, avoid a 50:50 balance of container to flower height. Flowers, opposite, are twice as wide as the vase.*

■ *Use florist foam, or oasis, to support stems arranged in low bowls.*

■ *Have a big event coming up? Practice arrangements with silk flowers. For two easy ones to try, see instructions on page 110.*

297-301

WHETHER YOU HAVE JUST A FEW MINUTES TO arrange flowers, an hour to trim a pillow, or an afternoon to sew a table skirt and decorative overskirt, you'll find the materials lists and all the step-by-step directions you need in this chapter. The projects, with techniques and page references, illustrate the how-tos for ideas featured throughout *Easy Style*. Use your own color preferences, fabric choices, and personal touches to make them uniquely your own. Alternative ideas and extra tips are given, too, to expand your choices.

SHORTCUTS TO EASY STYLE

Stitch pillows in a variety of sizes, update an old dresser with a stylish antiqued finish, unify a bath with leaf motifs stamped on plain fabrics, or stitch up lush draperies with unlined, inexpensive white cotton. A little time translates into a lot of look.

ROUND TABLECLOTH
WITH BURLAP OVERSKIRT

ROUND TABLECLOTH
(PAGE 6)

Newsprint (for pattern)

Straightedge

Pencil, thumbtack, and string
  (for a compass)

Bulletin-board cork or breadboard

Fabric

Matching sewing thread

Measure the tabletop diameter and divide in half. To this measurement, add the distance from the tabletop to the floor plus 1 inch. This is the tablecloth radius.

To prepare the pattern, tape pieces of newsprint together. With a straightedge, draw a line along one edge of the newsprint that measures twice the radius. Mark the center of the line. Cut a length of string several inches longer than the radius. Tie one end of the string around the pencil, then push the thumbtack through the other end of the string so the length measures the radius exactly. Push the tack through the center point marked on the newsprint and then into the cork board. Draw the half-circle pattern and cut out.

Fold the fabric in half. Place the straight edge of the pattern even with the fabric fold and cut out the circle. Note: If the fabric isn't wide enough to accommodate your pattern, use the full width of the fabric for the tablecloth center and stitch matching widths to each side of center width.

To hem the cloth, press under a ½-inch seam allowance around the fabric circle. Clip into the seam allowance so it lies flat. Press under ½ inch again and stitch.

BURLAP OVERSKIRT
(PAGE 6)

Burlap fabric

Fleece

Lining fabric

Piping to go around circumference of the tabletop (for self-covered cording)

Matching sewing thread

Buttons (one for each point on skirt edging)

Measure diameter of tabletop and add 1 inch. Prepare the pattern, then cut one shape each from burlap, fleece, and lining fabrics, as directed at left for round tablecloth. Baste fleece to the wrong side of burlap.

For the border, measure the circumference of the tabletop, using string. Draw a line the length of the string on newsprint. Draw your line parallel to the first line as the desired depth for the border. Connect the ends to make a rectangle. Draw a third line, lengthwise, down the center of the rectangle. Mark a dot at the beginning and the end of this line. Mark additional dots, evenly spaced, in between. Draw Vs, connecting the dots, to create a zigzag edge. Add ½-inch seam allowances along the zigzag edge, the sides, and the top edge. Cut out the pattern, then cut two shapes from the burlap.

With right sides facing, sew short ends of each burlap border together forming two rings. Sew rings together, right sides facing, along the zigzag edge. Clip into corners, trim points, and turn right side out. Press carefully, then baste along the top edge. Set the fabric piece aside.

Cut and piece 2-inch-wide bias strips of burlap to cover the piping cord. Fold the pieced strip in half lengthwise, wrong sides facing, around the piping cord and stitch in place using a zipper foot. Sew piping around the tablecloth top.

Sew the border to the tablecloth top with right sides facing. Clip into the seam allowance at even intervals.

Fold the border into the center of the tabletop. With right sides facing, sew the lining circle to the burlap circle, leaving an opening for turning. Clip into the seam allowance at even intervals, turn right side out, and press. Slip-stitch the opening closed.

PADDED INVITATION BOARD WITH POCKET

PADDED INVITATION BOARD WITH POCKET
(PAGE 6)

⅛-inch-thick wood (for the back)
Graph paper
Fleece
Striped cotton fabric
Thin cork board (for the front)
Staple gun
Ribbon
Upholstery tacks
Sawtooth metal picture hanger

Cut a rectangle from the ⅛-inch wood to the desired size of the finished invitation board. Draw around the wood rectangle onto graph paper and add ½-inch seam allowances all around. Cut two pieces from the striped fabric.

Draw a pocket rectangle onto graph paper. Extend the top edge of the pocket ½ inch at each side. Redraw the rectangle sides, slanting them from the bottom edge to the extended top edge. Draw a wavy line across the top edge of the pocket, then add ½-inch seam allowances all around. Cut two pockets from the striped fabric.

With right sides facing, sew the pockets together along the top edge. Note: If desired, stiffen the pocket with iron-on interfacing. Clip the wavy seam allowance at regular intervals, turn the pocket right side out, and press. Baste raw edges together. Place the pocket on top of one striped rectangle, matching the bottom raw edges. Stitch bottom edge. Sew the sides in the same manner, matching raw edges (the pocket will "pouch" out slightly). With right sides facing, sew the pocket rectangle to the remaining striped rectangle along the sides and top edge, using a scant

½-inch seam allowance. Clip corners and turn right side out. Slip the wood inside the fabric rectangle, turn the raw edges at the bottom edge, and slip-stitch the opening closed.

Draw a square onto graph paper about ⅜ inch narrower and shorter than the wood rectangle, then subtract the height of the finished pocket from the height of the paper shape. Cut out the pattern. Cut the pattern from fleece, then cut the shape from striped fabric, adding a 1½-inch seam allowance all around. Lay the fabric, right side down, on a flat surface. Center the fleece, then the cork shape, on top of the fabric. Wrap the excess fabric over the sides to the back of the cork. Staple in place. Turn

the shape to the right side.

Cross pieces of ribbon over the front, pinning them in place. Staple ribbon ends to the wrong side of the cork. Place the beribboned shape in place on the front of the pocketed shape. Nail upholstery tacks through the ribbon at the intersections, into the board, and into the wood of the pocketed shape.

To finish the piece, nail a sawtooth metal picture hanger on the back of the piece for hanging. Slip notes, tickets, and correspondence under ribbon and into the pocket.

BASIC PILLOW

EASY STYLE
(PAGE 8)

Graph paper and pencil
Pillow form or polyester fiberfill
Fabric for the pillow front and back
Matching sewing thread

Determine the finished size for your pillow. Draw the shape onto graph paper. Add ½ inch all around for seam allowances. Using the graph-paper pattern, cut out a pillow front and a back from fabric.

With right sides facing, sew the pillow front to the back, leaving an opening along one edge for inserting the pillow form. Clip corners and curves, if necessary. Insert pillow form and slip-stitch the opening closed.

DRAPERIES

DRAPERIES FROM SHEETS
(PAGE 11)

Two flat, patterned sheets per
  window (two full size work for
  a standard, double-hung
  window)
Matching thread
Drapery rod sized to your window
  or tension rod

Measure your windows to determine the size sheet you'll need. They look best when each of the two panels is about twice the width of the window. For standard windows, two full-size flat sheets will work. If you like the look of fabric puddling on the floor, you'll need about 6 to 8 extra inches for the desired effect. (This will affect how high you can hang your panels.)

For an easy treatment, use the bottom hem as casing for the rod and allow the decorative edge to puddle. Add ribbons or raffia for tie-backs or stitch your own from a pillowcase.

SPECIALTY PILLOWS

FRINGE-TRIMMED PILLOWS
(PAGE 12)

Jute bouillon fringe
Plus all materials for basic pillow,
  shown at left

Purchase or sew decorative pillows. To sew a pillow, see sewing directions for basic pillow, left. Before joining the back to the front, sew fringe to pillow front with right sides facing.

Thick fringes (or cording or other decorative trims) can be hand-sewn around the outside edge of a finished cover (see photo at right). Carefully measure around the outer edge of the pillow and add 2 inches. Cut trim to this measurement. Pin in place, and overcast to the seam.

For a timesaver, hot-glue decorative trim to a purchased pillow. Test your technique with an old pillow and cheap trim to make sure no glue shows. Or, simply hot-glue a decorative (blazer) crest as trim for a purchased velvet pillow.

BUTTON-TRIMMED FLAP
(PAGE 14)

Graph paper
Fabric for the flap
Matching sewing thread
Ready-made pillow
Four large buttons

Draw a square for the flap pattern onto graph paper. Add ½ inch for seam allowances. Cut out a front and matching back from fabric.

With right sides facing, sew the squares together, leaving an opening for turning. Clip corners, turn right side out, and press. Insert pillow. Slip-stitch opening closed (see photo at right). Pin flap diagonally to the pillow front. Sew a button in each corner to hold flap in place.

FURNITURE FINISHES—
DISTRESSED AND WASHED

DISTRESSED FINISH
FOR DRESSER WITH LARGE
GOLD STARS
(PAGE 13)

Commercial paint stripper
(if necessary)
Medium-grade sandpaper
Cotton rags
Medium to dark latex paint
Nylon paint brush
Optional: Stencil, stencil paints

If painted, use a commercial stripper to remove paint. Follow technique and safety instructions. Sand and wipe clean with a damp cloth. If stained, follow the sanding suggestions for the color wash finish. Paint dresser with a medium- to dark-colored latex paint. When dry, lightly sand base coat to a dull finish; wipe clean. For the top coat mix equal amounts of white latex paint and water together. Paint the entire dresser and let sit for 20 minutes. Using a circular motion, lightly wipe away paint with a clean cloth. For the distressed look, wipe away more of the top coat in the center of the doors and less around the edges of the dresser. When the paint is completely dry, hand-paint or stencil stars with a metallic-finish paint. For easy application, use a liquid acrylic, paint cream, or paint stick formulated for stenciling and handpainted detailing.

ALTERNATIVE FINISH
WOOD COLOR WASHES
(NOT SHOWN)

Medium-grain sandpaper
Cotton rags
Medium to dark latex paint

Before colorwashing, remove drawers from dresser; then remove knobs from drawers. Using medium-grain sandpaper, sand the piece, if stained, to roughen the stained finish and remove shine. Wipe clean with a damp cloth. To colorwash, mix three parts of medium- to dark-colored latex paint with one part water. Apply paint to drawers and body following the direction of the wood grain. Let sit for 10 minutes, then lightly rub along the wood grain with a clean cloth. For a darker colorwash, apply a second paint coat and let sit for 20 minutes before removing surface paint.

BEDROOM HEADBOARD

UPHOLSTERED HEADBOARD
(PAGE 17)

½-inch plywood
(for the headboard)
Tightly woven cotton or cotton-blend
fabric
High-loft quilt batting
Staple gun
Two 1 × 4s
Bolts, washers, screws, portable
hand drill (to attach headboard
to bed frame)

Measure the width of your bed and determine the desired height of the headboard (our example is about 24 inches tall). Cut shape from plywood. Measure the height of your bed and add the height of the headboard. Cut the 1 × 4s to this measurement.

Cut one piece of fabric the shape of the plywood for the backing. Then cut a piece of batting (or several pieces of batting, depending on the desired thickness of the padding) and another piece of fabric to cover the front of the plywood. Add at least 4 inches to each side for wrapping the fabric/batting around the edges.

Lay the front fabric, right side down, on a flat surface and cover with the batting. Center the plywood on top. Fold the excess fabric and batting smoothly around the edges and staple to the back of the plywood

Press under the raw edges of the backing fabric 1 inch all around. Staple the backing in place, keeping the fabric taut.

Paint the 1 × 4s in a color to match the fabric. Screw the 1 × 4s to the wrong side of each edge of the headboard frame.

Drill holes for bolts though each 1 × 4. Fasten headboard to the bed rail with bolts and washers.

ANTIQUED DRESSER FINISH

ANTIQUED PALE FINISH WITH SMALL STARS
(PAGE 23)

Commercial paint stripper
(if necessary)
Cotton rags
Sandpaper
Light cream or yellow latex paint
Nylon paintbrush
Flat-finish varnish
Round stippling brush
Optional: Stencils, stencil paints

Remove paint and sand dresser smooth as for distressed finish. Paint dresser with a light cream or yellow paint and let dry. Working in one area at a time, apply a light-colored varnish on top of the base coat in a crisscrossed manner. With a stippling brush (from an art store or stencil supplier), firmly push the bristles into the wet varnish to create a dappled effect. Then hold the brush flat against the surface and pull the brush along the direction of the wood grain. As an alternative, stencil or hand-paint stars over the thoroughly dry surface.

WINDOW DRESSINGS

UNLINED COTTON DRAPERY PANELS
(PAGE 28)

Lightweight fabric

Matching thread

Rubber O-rings (one for each decorative S-hook)

Iron rod and decorative iron S-hooks

Measure the wall from the ceiling to the floor and add about 12 inches for the curtain puddle. Measure width of the window and multiply 2½ times.

Cut the necessary length of fabric yardage. Cut additional lengths, piecing them together at the sides to achieve the desired width. If desired, turn under ¼ inch twice on all sides of the fabric and hem.

Mark the top edge at even intervals (about 24 inches apart). Pinch the fabric at the first mark between your fingers. Lift up the fabric. With the finger of your other hand, squeeze the fabric into a length of about 9 inches. Fold the 9 inches in half; slip the O-ring over the top fold and down about 1½ inches. Repeat across the top. Place S-hooks over mounted rod, then slip the looped fabric over the ends of the S-hooks

BEDROOM FLORAL ARRANGEMENT

HANGING A DRIED FLOWER GARLAND
(PAGE 22)

Wire

Nails

Screw eyes

Create a small hanging loop from wire at the top of the garland, wrapping the wire around branches of the garland's grapevine base. Hang the garland from a nail hammered into the headboard.

To steady the ends of an especially long garland, attach screw eyes into the headboard. Wrap wire through the screw eyes and through the grapevine. Note: If the surface of the door or headboard is dimensional like ours, be careful not to pull the wire too tight. Instead, leave a little space between the headboard and the garland so the garland doesn't bend.

SPECIALITY FINISH

CRACKLE FINISH
(PAGE 47)

Painted or unfinished chest
Liquid sander
Sandpaper
Sanding sealer
Primer
Emerald green and light green
  latex paint
Hide glue
Nylon paintbrush
Polyurethane varnish

If your chest is painted, you don't have to strip off the original paint for this technique. Instead, paint it with a coat of liquid sander. For an unfinished chest, sand the wood, then seal it with a coat of sanding sealer. Paint with primer. When dry, paint the base coat with emerald green and allow to dry again.

For the crackle finish, mix two parts hide glue to one part water in a disposable container. Using a nylon brush and long strokes, apply the glue mixture. Rinse out the brush as soon as you've finished using it. Let the glue mixture dry overnight.

Apply a coat of light green over the chest. Do not brush over an area that is already painted. The paint will begin to crack in about 20 seconds. Allow to dry overnight.

Finish with one or two coats of polyurethane varnish.

Alternative: Use commercially available acrylic crackle glaze or crackle varnish if available and carefully follow the directions. Always seal with clear varnish for protection.

SCREEN GEMS

PHOTO SCREEN
(PAGE 47)

Plywood panels (see below)
Medium-grit sandpaper
Paint in your desired shade
Roller
Paint brush
4 piano hinges
Matching wood photo frames
  (8 ×10)
Picture hangers and
  finishing nails

Have three pieces of ¾-inch paint-grade plywood cut into 20-inch × 6-foot sections. Sand smooth with medium-grit sandpaper. Wipe clean with damp cloth. Paint all sides of wood with three coats of stain and allow to dry. Using piano hinges, attach screen panels together accordion-style at top and bottom of panels. Frame 8 × 10 photos in matching wood frames. Lay screen flat and center frames on front as desired. Once placement is determined, accurately center each frame by measuring from top and sides of each screen panel. Nail picture hangers to frame; stand screen up, hang photos.

BATHROOM IMPRESSIONS

LEAF STAMPS
(PAGES 50 AND 51)

Fresh leaves or dry leaves treated
with glycerine (from crafts store)
¼-inch foam-core board
Crafts knife; extra knife blades
Double-stick tape
Paint in your choice of color or
colors (type depends on project;
see pages 50-51)
Artist brush

Trace your leaves, smooth side down, onto ¼-inch foam-core board. Maple, oak, and ash are good choices for graphic shapes.

Cut out the leaf shapes with a crafts knife. Change blades often to keep the edges of the cut foam-core smooth and even.

Use double-stick tape to fasten each leaf to its foam-core board shape. Place the smooth, nonveined side of the leaf against the board.

Paint the leaves with a thin coat of paint. Too much paint will muddy the veins and destroy detail. Wash the leaf as needed to remove paint. Or, replace as needed.

Press the wet leaf to the wall or fabric, being careful not to twist or slide. Carefully pull it away and repeat the process.

When paint is dry, fill any blank areas with a second hue. Apply it lightly and randomly with a brush or sponge for a natural effect.

DECOUPAGED DRAWER FRONTS
(PAGE 53)

Maps

White glue

Paintbrush

Decoupage varnish or polyurethane

Measure the drawer fronts and cut matching shapes from maps. Note: Cut the shapes from unfolded portions of map whenever possible. Use a warm iron to carefully press wrinkles from maps, if necessary.

Thin glue with water to the consistency of light cream. Brush drawer with glue, then apply the map cutout. Let dry.

Seal with several coats of decoupage varnish or polyurethane.

KIDS' FITTED SPREAD
(PAGE 53)

Prequilted fabric

Matching sewing thread

Measure the width and length of the mattress top and add ½ inch for seam allowances. Measure the depth and length of each side. To each of the side measurements, add 1 inch to the depth, then add seam allowances all around the edges.

Cut out one top and four sides from the prequilted fabric.

With right sides facing and using ½-inch seam allowance, sew short edges of each side piece together, creating a large ring. Press seams open.

Sew the fabric top to the upper edge of the ring, placing the corners of the top even with the seam lines. Turn under ½ inch twice at the bottom of the raw edge.

BASEBALL AND BAT HEADBOARD (PAGE 53)

Plywood cut to fit
  (see directions below)
Jigsaw
Finishing nails
Paintbrushes
Fine art brush for detailing

For ball and bat sides, cut two 1 × 6-inch wood planks 55 inches long. Center and draw a 5-inch-diameter ball at one end of each plank. Referring to photograph, draw outline of bat under ball, tapering slightly to resemble bat. Using a jigsaw, cut around the ball and bat. From 1 × 6-inch wood planks, cut four center pickets 50 inches long. (You'll need to cut six or seven for a full-size bed, depending on spacing.) Cut points at one end for pickets. Or, look for pre-cut pickets in the size you need at lumber store. Smooth all rough edges with sandpaper. Cut two 1 × 3-inch wood boards the same width as the bed frame. Lay supports 12 inches apart on a flat surface. Position ball and bat pieces on each end and center pickets in between; nail in place. Paint bats and pickets as desired. Paint balls white, adding brown stitching with a fine paintbrush.

FLORAL INTERESTS

DRIED FLOWERS AND HATS WALL ARRANGEMENT (PAGE 57)

Commercial mirror
L-hooks or Shaker pegs
Dried flowers and leaves
Plastic foam arch (base for dried-flower arrangement)
Glue gun and hotmelt adhesive
Floral pin and an L-hook (for hanging)

Hang the mirror so that it reflects a pretty picture of the room.

Plan the arrangement of the hats and screw L-hooks or pegs into the wall and into the mirror frame to display them.

Plan the arrangement of dried flowers on the foam base. Use flowers and leaves that are varied in shape and size for the most interesting impact. This composition is symmetrical, worked around three major clusters of flowers, the brightest one in the center and two lighter-colored clusters at each end. Push the stems of the flowers (except for those that are especially delicate) into the foam first, adding hotmelt adhesive where necessary. Fill in with leaves, then finish with the most delicate flowers.

To hang the arrangement, push a floral pin into the back of the foam, leaving about ½ inch of the pin exposed. Cover the pin where it enters the foam with hotmelt adhesive. Hang the arrangement from an L-hook screwed into the wall.

To hang a grapevine-based arrangement, create a sturdy ring of wire on the upper back of the grapevine. Hang the wire over a picture hook.

FLOWERS: TWO ARRANGEMENTS TO TRY

Silk flowers (to practice)
Florist foam or oasis
Fresh flowers (lilacs and echium)
Sphagnum moss
Greenery (such as boxwood)
Florist shears
Crafts knife
Container

Informal: Use silk flowers to practice. Mix rigid, soft, straight, curved, or drooping flowers with silk greenery. Pair texture for drama; combine textures for formality. Cut a foam block to snugly fit the container. Cut the flowers to the desired length. (When in doubt, leave them long.) Place the strongest flowers in the center. (Size, color, and shape determine visual strength.) Bend the stems of silk flowers for a natural look.

Fill in with flowers that cascade over the side, other large blossoms, and accent flowers. Arrange fully for a lush look. When you are satisfied, take a snapshot so you can easily re-create with fresh flowers if you desire. Or, make a silk arrangement and fill in with fresh flowers as the seasons change. Just a few fresh flowers enliven a permanent arrangement.

Formal: For a pleasing look, gather flowers from the same color family—here pale peach roses to saffron freesia. Depending on the height of your container, cut stems to stagger as shown. Cut and arrange freesia stems so they arch gracefully over the container. For a bridal shower, combine white or palest pink flowers.

EASY STYLE CONTRIBUTORS

Page 5 Design by Eddie Nunns, Dallas, Texas; photography: Colleen Duffley, Dallas, Texas.

Pages 6-23 Design by Chapman Design, Houston, Texas; photography: Fran Brennan, Houston, Texas.

Pages 24-29 Design by Two Women Boxing, Dallas, Texas; photography: Colleen Duffley.

Pages 32-35 Design by John Wiltgen, Chicago, Illinois; photography: James Yochum, Sawyer, Michigan/Tucson, Arizona.

Living room (pages 32-33 photo B): Furnishings: sofa and chair: Quatrine, Chicago; rug: Pottery Barn (800-922-5507); round end table, cocktail table, urns, gilded mirror, table lamp: Ethan Allen (800-228-9229); metal chairs, floor lamps: Mario Villa Gallery, New Orleans, Louisiana; pillows, throw: Arrelle Fine Linens, Chicago.

Dining room (pages 34-35 photo B): table base: Jay Robert's Antique Warehouse, Chicago; chairs: Ethan Allen; pots: Elements Inc., Chicago; Topiaries: Chicagoblooms, Chicago.

Pages 32-35 Design by Terri Weinstein, Chicago, Illinois; photography: James Yochum.

Living room (page 34 photo A): sofa, chair: Quatrine; table, metal vase: Jayson Home & Garden, Chicago; Table with window top: Ancient Echoes, Chicago; Table and lamp: Luminaire, Chicago; vases: Elements Inc., Chicago; kilim: Minasian Oriental Rugs, Chicago;

curtain rods and finials: Calico Corners (800-777-9933); painting: Mario Villa Gallery.

Dining room (page 32 photo A): table base: Jay Robert's; bentwood chairs: Luminaire; plate stand: Sawbridge Studios, Chicago; Candlesticks, ladder: Decoro, Chicago; glasses, bowls on shelves, throw: Tabula Tua, Chicago; rug: Pottery Barn; painting: Mario Villa.

Pages 32-35 Design by Marc Straits, Chicago, Illinois; photography by James Yochum.

Living room (page 33 photo C): chair, large pot: The Golden Triangle, Chicago; glass bowl, tan pillow: Sawbridge Studios, Chicago; blue pillow fabric: Loomcraft, Vernon Hills, Illinois; rug: Oriental Rugs International, Chicago.

Dining room (page 35, photo C): table: Jay Robert's; bamboo shades, woven floor mat, basket on table: Pier 1 Imports (800-447-4371); fabric treatment: Loomcraft.

Page 42-43 Design by Barbara Hawthorn, Barbara Hawthorn Interiors, McLean, Virginia; photography: Gordon Beall, Washington, D.C.

Page 46-47 Design by Chapman Design; photography: Fran Brennan.

Page 52 Design by Barbara Hawthorn; photography: Gordon Beall.

Page 53 Design by Chapman Design; photography: Fran Brennan.

Page 54-55 Design by Peggy Pepper, Dallas; photography: Colleen Duffley.

Page 75 Design by Eddie Nunns; photography: Colleen Duffley.

Page 78 Design by Jan Barboglio, Dallas; photography: Colleen Duffley.

Page 94 Design by Joetta Moulden, Houston; photography: Hal Lott, Houston.

INDEX

U.S. UNITS TO METRIC EQUIVALENTS		
To Convert From	**Multiply By**	**To Get**
Inches	25.4	Millimeters (mm)
Inches	2.54	Centimeters (cm)
Feet	30.48	Centimeters (cm)
Feet	0.3048	Meters (m)

METRIC UNITS TO U.S. EQUIVALENTS		
To Convert From	**Multiply By**	**To Get**
Millimeters	0.0394	Inches
Centimeters	0.3937	Inches
Centimeters	0.0328	Feet
Meters	3.2808	Feet